Junior Science

seeds

Terry Jennings

Illustrations by David Anstey

Gloucester Press
New York · London · Toronto · Sydney

About this book

You can learn many different things about seeds in this book. There are lots of experiments and activities for you to try. You will find out what seeds are, what they grow into and how seeds are formed. You can also find out about what seeds need to grow, what is inside a seed, how and why seeds are scattered and much more.

First published in the
United States in 1988 by
Gloucester Press
387 Park Avenue South
New York, NY 10016

ISBN 0 531 17087 X

Library of Congress Catalog
Card Number: 87-82973

© BLA Publishing Limited 1988

This book was designed and produced by BLA Publishing Limited, TR House, Christopher Road, East Grinstead, Sussex, England.

A member of the Ling Kee Group
London Hong Kong Taipei Singapore New York
Printed in Spain by Heraclio Fournier, S.A.

Seeds grow into plants. There are lots of different kinds of seeds. Some seeds grow into vegetables and some become flowers. A cabbage seed will grow into a cabbage plant and a poppy seed will grow into a poppy plant. Many stores sell seeds in packets.

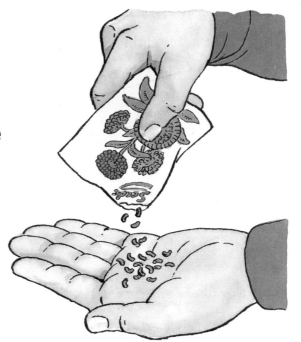

Try growing a pea plant from a pea seed. Plant the pea seed in a pot of earth and water it well.

After a while a shoot will appear. When the plant has grown bigger, white flowers will grow on the pea plant. When the flowers die, pea pods will form. Inside the pea pods there are peas.

You can find out more about seeds by looking closely at a bean seed. Soak some bean seeds in water and then split one of the seeds open.

Inside the seed you will see a tiny plant. Around the plant is the food it needs to grow. All seeds have a tiny plant and all seeds have some food.

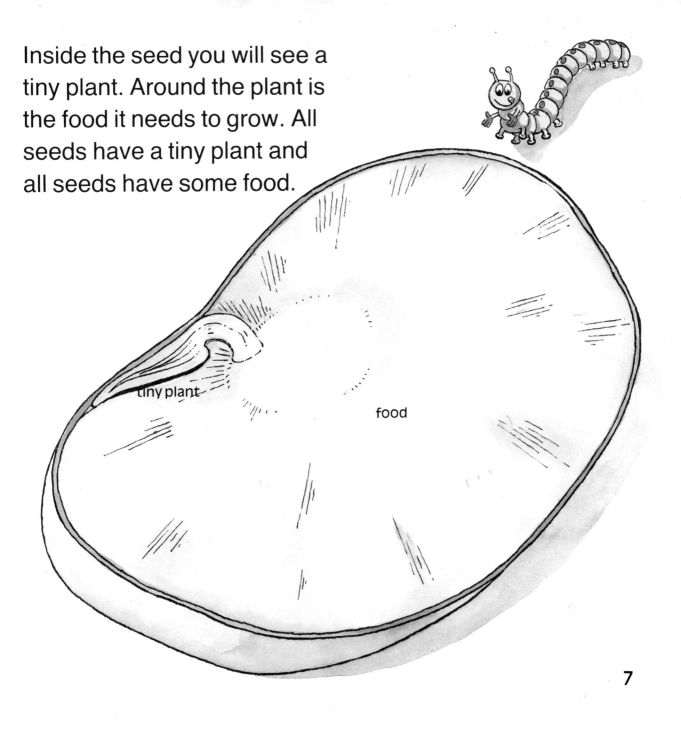

tiny plant

food

7

Plant a bean seed in a jar like this. The bean root will grow first. It grows down. Then a shoot will grow. It grows up.

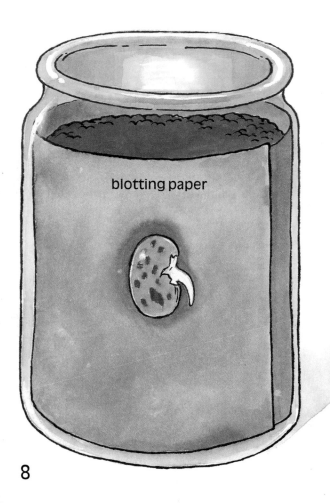

blotting paper

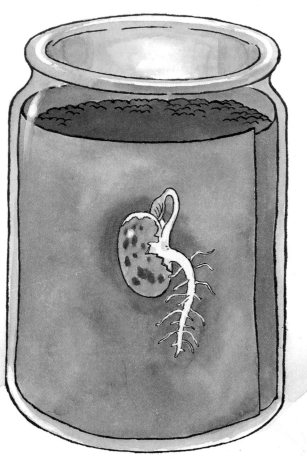

The plant will grow bigger. If you put it in a pot you can keep it for a long time. It will grow flowers from which bean pods will form.

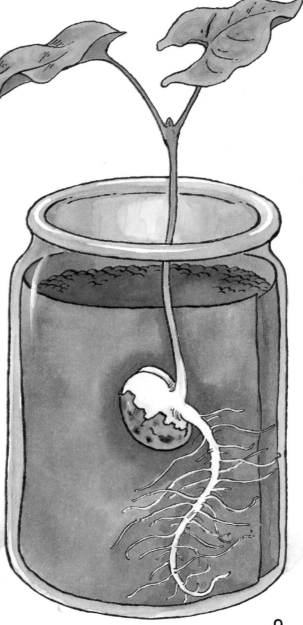

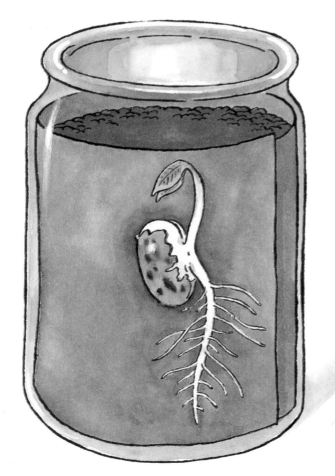

Seeds need water to grow. You can see this for yourself. Take two eggshells. In one eggshell put some wet cotton. In the other put dry cotton. Sprinkle a few cress seeds on each.

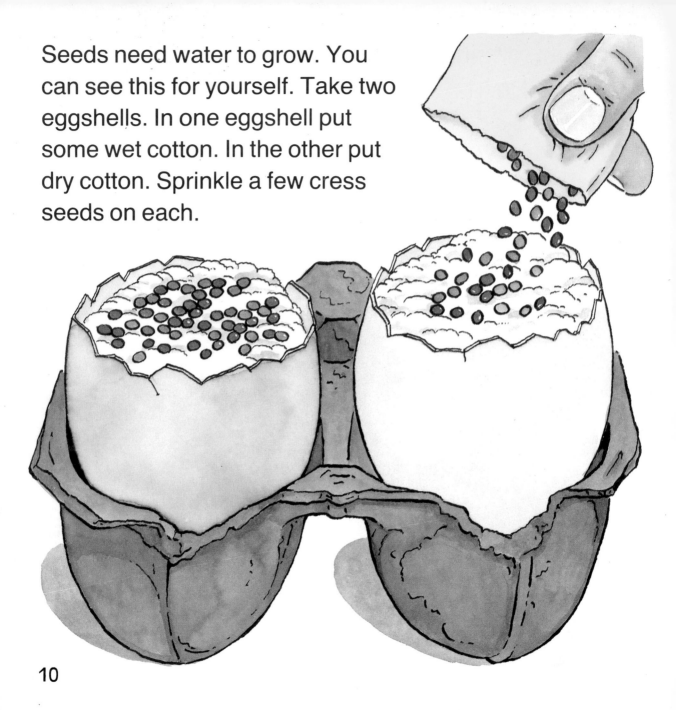

Draw faces on the eggshells and put them by the window. After a few days the eggshell with the wet cotton will sprout cress plant "hair." The seeds on the dry cotton will not grow.

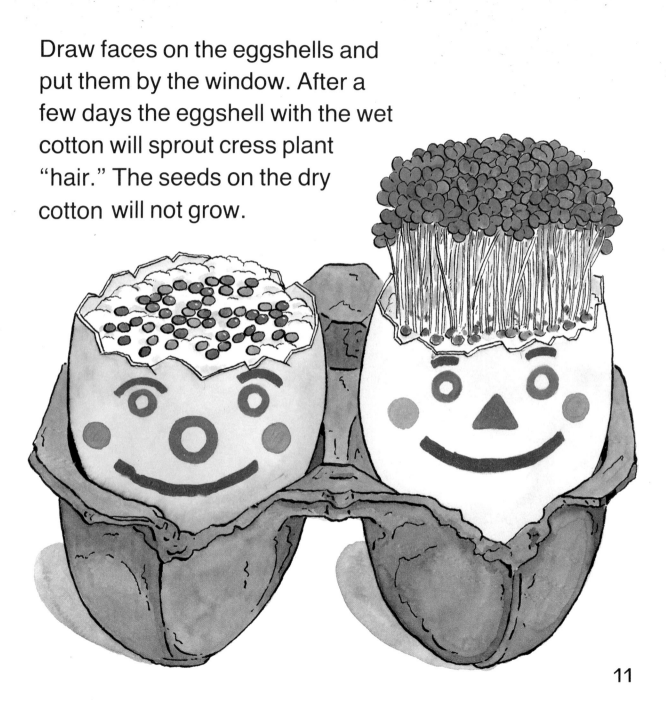

Seeds must be scattered. If they are not
scattered they will grow too close together.
Then the plants will not be strong.

Birds eat juicy fruits like berries. They drop the seeds far away from the plant that made them. This helps to scatter seeds.

These are all juicy fruits. Plums, peaches and cherries have hard seed coverings called stones. The seeds are inside the stones. The other fruits in the picture have pips. The pips are seeds.

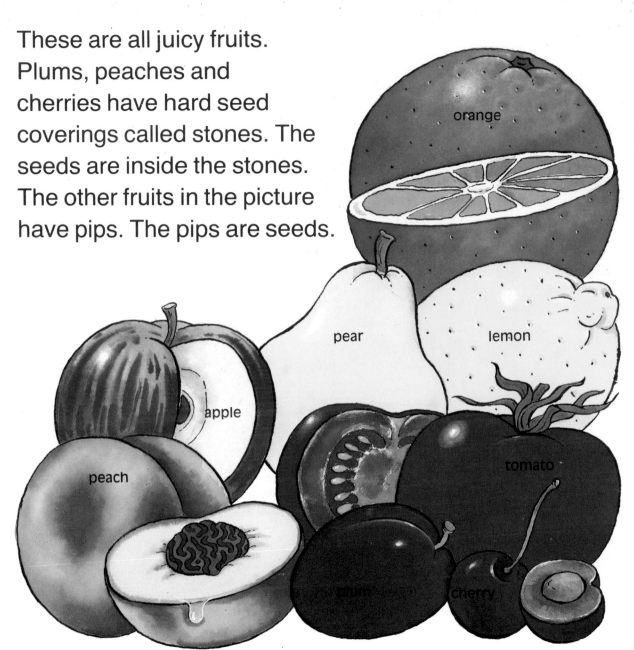

orange

pear

lemon

apple

peach

tomato

plum

cherry

14

Not all fruits are juicy. Nuts are dry fruits. The seed of the chestnut tree is inside the chestnut. The seed of the oak is the acorn. Some animals help to scatter seeds. Mice and squirrels hide nuts and acorns for the winter. They often forget where they left them. The nuts and acorns then grow.

Some fruits have little hooks. The hooks cling to the coats of animals when they brush against the plant. They also cling to people's clothing. In this way the seeds are scattered.

Some fruits burst open. The pea pod is the fruit of the pea plant. When pea seeds are ripe and hard the pea pod bursts open. When the pod opens the seeds scatter.

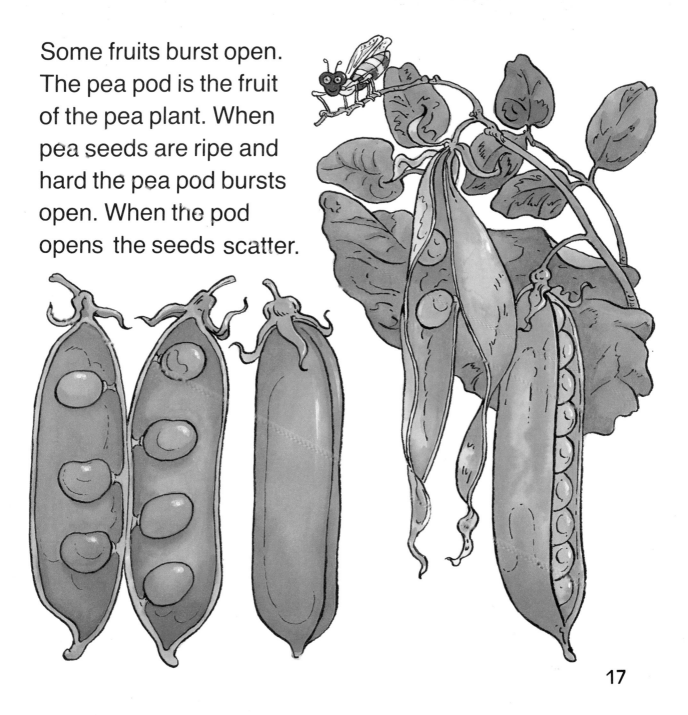

Some fruits have hairs. Dandelion "clocks" are made up of lots of dandelion fruits. Each fruit has a tiny parachute. The parachute is a tuft of hairs. The tiny parachutes float away in the wind. They carry the dandelion fruits away from the plant.

Other fruits have "wings." The fruits of the maple tree have wings. When the wind blows, the wings help to carry the fruits away from the tree which made them. The seeds are scattered and so the new trees will have room to grow.

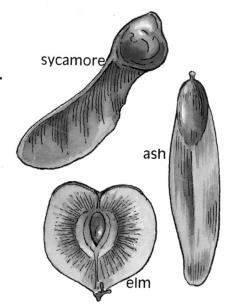

sycamore

ash

elm

A few seeds are scattered by water. Waterlily fruits float on water. They float to a new part of the pond, lake or river. The seeds are scattered. Coconuts float on the sea to new places.

Many of the foods we eat are made from seeds. Flour is made from wheat seeds. Bread, cookies and noodles are made from flour. All of the foods in the picture either contain seeds or have been made from seeds.

coffee

rice

pepper

mustard

cocoa

spaghetti

cereals

maize or sweetcorn

Imagine how many pips there must be on this apple tree. But they don't all grow into new trees. Birds, animals and people eat the apples. And pips may fall in places where they can't grow.

glossary

Here are the meanings of some words you may have used for the first time in this book.

berry: a small fruit containing seeds.

fruit: the part of a plant that contains the seeds.

nut: a dry fruit with a hard shell.

pip: a seed of some juicy fruits like oranges.

pod: a long green fruit containing seeds.

root: the part of a plant which grows into the ground.

scatter: to throw or move things in all directions.

seed: a small part of a plant that can grow into a new plant.

shoot: the young tip of a growing plant.

index